Always Do
The Best
yo can
Be

Being
DIFFERENT
is OKAY

2024

About the Author:

Born and raised in Brooklyn, Shamika Rose Cousar-Arquee is a minister, author and motivational speaker with twenty-one years of experience in ministry and twenty-five working as a School Safety Agent in New York City public schools. She is a daughter, sister, wife, and caretaker for her longtime furry friend Mello.

Whether in NYC schools or in the community at large, Shamika has a passion for using her voice and her experiences to guide others to be successful in their spiritual journeys. She received a Bachelors in Psychology from Brooklyn College, a Masters in Divinity from New York Theological Seminary, and a Doctorate in Pastoral Theology from Anchor Theological Seminary and Bible Institute. Being Different is Okay is her first childrens book, inspired by her own childhood journey towards self-acceptance. Her first book Live Undefeated (2014) is a guide towards spiritual fulfillment for adults. Finally, Shamika released an album Stepping Out on Faith (2017).

About the Illustrator:

I am Marya Litvinna, I am an illustrator of children's literature and I created the illustrations for this marvellous book. My mission is to teach young readers to notice the beauty around us, to love and respect themselves, as well as other people. I hope my illustrations will help the audience to treat themselves gently and with love!

For information regarding author interviews, please contact
shamikaarquee@gmail.com

CHAPTER ONE

Kamanie had a heart as bright as the sun, but there was a tiny cloud that followed her around. Kamanie cared a lot about what other people thought. She didn't like going out much because she was worried about everything: what she looked like, what she wore, how she talked, and even her hair.

Kamanie's room was her safe haven, like an enchanted castle where she could be herself. She'd stand in front of the mirror, her eyes filled with doubt.

"Am I enough?" she'd ask herself, her voice as soft as a whisper. Her reflection looked back, waiting for an answer.

Outside her window, kids played with joyful laughter, like characters in a storybook. But Kamanie hesitated to join them. She'd look at her clothes and frown. "What if they laugh at my outfit?" She worried.

One sunny morning, her mom called from downstairs, "Kamanie, it's time to get ready for school!"

Kamanie's heart skipped a beat. School meant facing more questions, more doubts, and more worries. She sighed, her room echoing with the sound.

As she stared at her closet, Kamanie wished for a mystical outfit that could make her feel confident and strong. She picked out a dress she liked, but then thought, *Maybe it's too bright. Maybe I'll wear jeans.* Then she changed her mind again, *But what if everyone else is wearing something else?*

Kamanie looked in the mirror, her reflection looking back at her with a puzzled expression. "What's wrong with me?" she whispered.

Her mom knocked on the door. "Kamanie, you need to head to school soon!"

Kamanie sighed and picked something out, even though her heart wasn't convinced. She looked in the mirror one more time before leaving her room. "I wish I could be confident like the kids outside," she thought.

CHAPTER TWO

One day, as Kamanie walked to school with her head down, something caught her eye. It was a bright flier pinned to a bulletin board. It read, "Embrace Your Uniqueness Workshop."

Kamanie was curious. "Maybe this is what I need," she thought. So, with a brave heart, she signed up for the workshop.

The workshop was like stepping into a world of colors and dreams. Kids gathered around, their eyes shining like stars. A friendly woman with a warm smile stood at the front.

"Welcome, everyone!" she exclaimed. "Today, we're going to learn that it's okay to be different."

As the workshop began, Kamanie listened carefully. The woman talked about how each person is like a puzzle piece, and when we all come together, we create something beautiful. "Our differences are what make us unique," she said.

Kamanie's heart stirred. *Could it really be okay to be different?* She looked around the room and saw kids nodding, just like her.

The woman handed out little cards with words on them. Kamanie's card read, "Confident." The woman explained that these were words of affirmation, which are special words that could help them feel brave and strong.

As she read, Kamanie found herself humming a tune. The melody came to her, gentle and clear, like a flower carried in the wind. "I'm strong, I'm kind, I'm awesome, that's true. I'll be myself, there's no one like you."

It was like a little spark ignited within her. *Could these words really change how she felt about herself?* She decided to give it a try, to see if the magic worked for her.

That night, Kamanie sat on her bed, her card in her hand. "Confident," she whispered to herself. She sang it to herself like a secret song, feeling a tiny spark of courage. She went to stand in front of the mirror, and she saw herself in a new light. "Confident," she sang again, her voice growing stronger.

Kamanie began to practice her words of affirmation every day. At first, it felt strange to say kind things to herself. But with every repetition, the words started to feel soft and warm like the hugs her mother would give her whenever she needed comfort or encouragement.

FABULOUS
OPTIMISTIC
I AM ENOUGH!
FUNNY
CONFIDENT
BEAUTIFUL
LOVE YOURSELF
KIND
FEARLESS
STRONG
BRAVE
LEADER
UNSTOPPABLE
INTELLIGENT

CHAPTER THREE

As the days went by, Kamanie's confidence grew. She realized that everyone had their own worries and doubts, just like she did. And with her words of affirmation, she felt like a warrior, a warrior whose shield was her courage.

One day, Kamanie saw a group of kids huddled together, whispering and laughing. She felt a pang of unease. "What if they're talking about me?" she thought.

But then, like a burst of fireworks, Kamanie remembered her newfound strength. She whispered her words of affirmation. They made her heart as steady as a drumbeat.

Deep inside, Kamanie had come to believe that being different was her strength. She had discovered the secret that when you believe in yourself, the whole world sees the amazing person you are.

That night, as Kamanie was flipping through her favorite storybook that is filled with colorful illustrations, a page fell open to a wondrous forest. It was filled with vibrant, mismatched creatures — a pink elephant, a purple giraffe, and a green zebra. As she looked at the page, something inside excited her.

"These animals are so different, but they look so happy!" Kamanie whispered to herself. The thought of being different no longer seemed scary; it seemed exciting, like an adventure waiting to be discovered.

As Kamanie lay in her bed, staring up at the glow-in-the-dark stars on her ceiling, she made a decision. "Tomorrow," she promised herself, "I'm going to step out into the world, just as I am. I'll be different, and that's okay."

CHAPTER FOUR

The next morning, Kamanie woke up feeling something magical in the air. The sun was shining so bright and the birds were singing a happy tune. The smell of her mom's tasty bacon and eggs filled the room.

The aroma had traveled from downstairs in the kitchen and found its way in her bedroom circling round and round until the scent went straight up her nose.

Yum, bacon and eggs! Kamanie thought, jumping out of bed with a big smile. She was all set to start her day and get ready for school. So she popped out of the bed to wash up and brush her teeth. With a little pep in her step, Kamanie recited the song that had been growing like a garden in her heart and mind.

"I'm not worried about anything, they can say what they want to say. But today: I'm gonna be brave, and I'm doing things my way," she sang, feeling extra excited. Normally, Kamanie color-coordinated her clothes, but today she decided she didn't feel like matching. As she danced around her room, she decided something cool.

"Today, I'll wear whatever I want," she said to herself, pulling out clothes from her drawer. Instead of matching, she chose a red shirt, a green skirt, and even yellow socks! With a grin as bright as the sun, she picked up her blue hat and put on her white sneakers.

"Ta-da! I'm ready!" Kamanie declared, singing her song at the top of her lungs. "I'm not worried about a thing," she exclaimed, "Let them talk and I'll just sing! Today's the day I'm super brave, doing things in my own fun wave!"

Since attending the workshop, Kamanie had practiced this song millions of times. Sometimes, the words and the rhythm changed a little — but today, the phrasings were clear and the melody resounded in her heart. Bravery was now her sidekick, and she was going to rock the world in her own unique way!

CHAPTER FIVE

As Kamanie reached the bottom of the stairs and entered the kitchen. Even before her mom saw her, her mom shouted, "Someone's really happy today! You've got your happy shoes on today," her mom chuckled as Kamanie twirled around.

But when Mom turned and saw her, it was like Little Red Riding Hood meeting the big bad wolf at Grandma's house. Kamanie didn't know what had caused this reaction, but it was clear something extraordinary was happening.

Her mom jerked her head, trying to grab the toast before it popped out of the toaster, but it was too late. The toast rocketed up into the air, and Mom was left in shock.

Kamanie quickly asked, "Mom, are you okay? Mom, say something! Are you okay?"

Realizing her mom needed a moment, Kamanie decided not to overwhelm her with more questions. Instead, she went to the fridge, took out a carton of orange juice, and poured herself a glass. She grabbed a plate, piled it high with bacon and eggs, and said a quick grace before dusting off the fallen toast and slathering it with butter.

With a mouthful of delicious food, Kamanie couldn't help but blurt out, "Mom, this breakfast is like a dance party in my mouth! You're an amazing chef!" Her mom, still a bit stunned, managed a smile. It was clear that today was a day of surprises, and Kamanie was embracing every moment of it.

With a curious twist in her eye, Mom turned around and asked, "Are you feeling alright today?" Kamanie, still brimming with excitement, replied, "Absolutely! I'm fabulous! Why do you ask?"

Mom's eyebrows went up as she looked Kamanie over, her clothes a burst of colors, hair a little wild, and a bright blue winter hat on her head despite the warm weather. "It's 85 degrees outside, honey. You sure you're okay? You don't have a fever, do you?"

"No way, Mom, I don't have a fever! I'm as cool as a popsicle!" Kamanie reassured her.

"Well, let me take your temperature just in case," Mom said. She zoomed off to the bathroom like a flash, returning with the thermometer. She pulled Kamanie's head back, and flashing the thermometer like a maestro's baton or a magic wand, she commanded, "Open wide!"

Kamanie obeyed, and after a suspenseful moment, Mom declared, "No temperature here!"

CHAPTER SIX

Then, with a mix of concern and curiosity, Mom asked the million-dollar question: "So, what's with the wild, mismatched outfit, my little fashionista? You look like a rainbow explosion! Is everything alright?"

Kamanie giggled and shook her head, saying, "Mom, I feel awesome! This is seriously one of my best days ever!" She couldn't contain her happiness, spinning around and leaping into the air. "Today I'm being ME! I'm all about being different. Is there something wrong with being different?"

With a thoughtful look, Mom replied, "Well, there's absolutely nothing wrong with being different. But hey, how about throwing a little matching magic in there?" She chuckled, seeing Kamanie's one-of-a-kind style shining so bright.

"Mommy, I really don't want to change," Kamanie said earnestly. "I want to be different. Even if it means wearing colors that don't match. Being different is like having a secret treasure of fun, whether it's colors, clothes, or crazy hair! It feels like having a pair of wings that sets me free. I get to make choices that feel like me. And that's what I'm learning to do, just like you said I would one day. So, why not start now? Sometimes kids at school try to make everyone look the same, but I'm not going to follow that. I don't want to be like everyone else. There's something special about me, and I'll figure it out, but for now, I'm starting with my clothes."

Mom looked at Kamanie with a mix of pride and understanding. "My little star is growing up," Mom said softly.

Kamanie grinned back, saying, "You taught me to be me, Mom, and you don't have to worry. I'm good, just trying out some new things. You trust me, right?"

Mom's eyes twinkled. "Of course I do, Kamanie." Kamanie gave a determined nod. "Alright, then get ready for school!" Mom chuckled, a smirk playing on her lips.

With her orange juice in hand, Kamanie drained the last drop and headed for the door. "Have a wonderful day, Mom. I don't want to be late for school!" She swung open the door and called over her shoulder, "See you later, Mom!"

Just as she started down the walkway, she heard her mother's voice, "Kamanie, Kamanie! Have a fabulous day at school, sweetheart!" Kamanie turned around and waved, feeling like a superstar.

With her blue hat on, and with a skip in her step as she made her way to school, Kamanie chanted, "La-la-la, here comes the day! Gonna shine in my own way!"

Chapter Seven

As she walked to school, her heart felt lighter than a feather. She knew today was the day to stand tall, to be proud of who she was, and to show the world that being herself was the greatest adventure of all.

She felt something special brewing inside her. She realized that she was growing up, and this very day marked the start of something amazing. Today, she decided she wouldn't let anyone box her in. She was different, and she wanted to shine in her own dazzling way. What others said about her mismatched colors? Well, that just didn't matter.

In fact, Kamanie was doing something really big. She was making a decision that could shape her future. And guess what? She was ready to paint her own path, no matter what everybody else was up to. The "follow the crowd" game? Nope, not for her.

Kamanie whispered to herself, "Cool doesn't mean I have to match, because my personality isn't in my clothes. It's in me."

She strutted on, feeling a warm confidence. She knew she rocked whatever she wore, because she made it her own. And if someone didn't like her because of her clothes, well, that was okay too. It was like a friendship filter! Kamanie decided that if they couldn't see her awesomeness just because of what she had on, then maybe they weren't meant to be her buddies after all. She was becoming a master of her own journey, one bold step at a time.

Kamanie walked on, her thoughts as clear as a sunny day. She knew clothes couldn't tell her who someone really was. It was like reading the cover of a book without knowing the amazing story inside. "I have to get to know people just like I'd want them to know me," she thought, her determination shining through.

She prepared herself for any teasing that might come her way. Kamanie had her answer ready, like a warrior with her shield. "I look good, and you know what? You need to feel good too," she said with a grin. And then, she dropped a little truth bomb, "You should try it sometime. Being different is totally okay. I don't have to look like you or dress like you. I'm rocking just being me."

The thought that made Kamanie feel extra good was that we're all like puzzle pieces that fit together in the world. "God made us different and unique, just like a bunch of colorful puzzle pieces," she pondered. "So, embracing our uniqueness is like creating the most beautiful puzzle ever." She knew that if she let others pick her clothes, they might try to influence her thoughts and feelings too. But Kamanie was having none of that! She was the captain of her ship, sailing towards the horizon of her amazing, colorful adventure.

Chapter Eight

At last, Kamanie arrived at the school block and skipped into the playground, where the other kids were lined up to meet the teacher. As she approached her class, she noticed a group of kids huddled together, whispering and giggling while glancing in her direction. But Kamanie wasn't about to let that faze her. She paid it no mind and kept walking. She was determined to be brave.

She walked with purpose, her steps echoing courage. With her head held high and a smile as radiant as the sun, Kamanie walked on. She had decided that no one could rain on her parade. She didn't let the giggles and whispers get under her skin. Instead, she kept skipping forward, like a confident dancer moving to her own music. She was headed straight to where her classmates were lining up, ready to stand tall and show the world her true colors.

As Kamanie stepped up to the line, two students couldn't help but let their words float out, "Hey, look at Kamanie's mismatched clothes!" One of them added, "Those colors don't even match! She looks like a clown!" Their words hung in the air, followed by the sound of laughter from three others.

But right then, the teacher, like a superhero, spun around with a knowing smile. She asked loudly, "What's wrong with Kamanie's clothes?" Then, she turned the tables with her own encouraging words. "Kamanie's clothes are bright and beautiful like she just stepped out of a fantastical painting! Her yellow color is as bright as the sun. You know, the sun is shining so boldly today? And that blue hat is amazing like the sky above us. And green, like those strong and yummy veggies we eat, don't they make us strong? Oh, and don't forget red — like those brave fire trucks that firefighters ride in!"

The teacher's words wove a spell of understanding. "All these things have their own special colors. So why can't Kamanie have her own unique style?" She looked around, making sure everyone got the message. "Just because it's not what you'd wear doesn't give you the right to make fun of her. Being different is a wonderful thing! Maybe we should have a lesson about embracing our uniqueness." With that, she gave the signal to head indoors for class, like the conductor on a train ride to a new and wondrous place.

Kamanie felt so relieved when Mrs Keebler spoke up on her behalf. She felt like a cloud had lifted. It never feels good when classmates tease you, even if they think you're super strong. That warm feeling of being understood and supported was like a cozy blanket on a chilly day.

Chapter Nine

Inside the classroom, the teacher led everyone to gather around, like explorers around a treasure map. "Class, let's talk about being different!" she exclaimed with a twinkle in her eye. "Being unique is like having a treasure chest of special things about ourselves. Just like Kamanie's colorful clothes."

All eyes turned to Kamanie, who felt like the star of a dazzling show. "Kamanie here knows that being different is super cool, right?" Mrs. Keebler smiled.

Kamanie nodded, her heart shining. "Yep! Being different is what makes us all shine like the stars in the sky!"

A student named Timmy piped up, "But what if someone teases you like they made fun of Kamanie just a few minutes ago?"

Mrs. Keebler leaned in, like a wise wizard sharing a secret. "It's like this, Timmy. Imagine if all flowers were the same color, wouldn't the garden be boring? Our differences are what make us interesting and special."

Kamanie chimed in, "And if someone teases you, it's like they're missing out on a great adventure!"

Emma raised her hand shyly. "Sometimes, I'm scared to show people who I really am."

Mrs. Keebler patted her shoulder gently. "Oh, Emma, you're not alone. We all feel that way sometimes. But remember, being yourself is like a superpower. You'll find friends who love you for you!"

Now it was time to share stories, like adventurers around a campfire. Jason admitted he was shy sometimes, and Lily revealed she worried about her glasses. As they spoke, it felt like a cloud was being lifted from them all — the cloud of worrying that they had to be just like everyone else to be accepted.

After the lesson, Kamanie's classmates gathered around her, their eyes sparkling with newfound understanding. "Kamanie, we're really sorry about earlier. We get it now."

Kamanie beamed like a lighthouse on a starry night. "No worries! Friends support each other. Let's start fresh!"

Timmy hesitated, then asked, "Can you teach us how to be confident like you?"

Kamanie thought for a moment. "Sure thing! Every morning, I sing words of affirmation to myself. It's like a secret potion for confidence!"

Emma's eyes widened. "What are words of affirm-thingies?"

Kamanie giggled. "They're like happy magic spells you say to yourself. You can sing them too!"

So, in the middle of the classroom, they sang their affirmations together, like a chorus of brave adventurers. "I'm strong, I'm kind, I'm awesome, that's true! I'll be myself, there's no one like you!"

The whole class felt like a team, ready to conquer any challenge. And guess what? From that day on, they all recited their words of affirmation. Emma's shyness started to melt away, and Timmy stood a little taller. Lily wore her glasses as if they gave her eagle's eyes.

On the playground, Kamanie, Emma, Timmy, and Lily formed a circle of friends. They recited their affirmations together, feeling like they could touch the sky. "We're strong, we're kind, we're awesome, it's true! Being ourselves, there's no one like you!"

Kamanie's rainbow of confidence had spread, like colors on a painter's canvas. And as they skipped and laughed, the circle friends knew that being different was the greatest gift they could receive. They had become a team of explorers, embracing their uniqueness, and ready to face every new adventure with smiles on their faces and courage in their hearts.

Chapter Ten

As the days turned into weeks and the weeks into months, Kamanie's confidence continued to soar higher. She no longer worried about what others thought, because she knew her worth. Her heart felt as light as a feather, carrying her dreams high above the clouds.

One sunny afternoon, there was a festival at the park. Kamanie decided to join the festivities with her friends by her side. As they visited the colorful booths and played exciting games, Kamanie felt a sense of belonging she had never experienced before.

Another group of kids approached her, their faces bright with enthusiasm. "Hey, Kamanie, we're putting on a talent show! Will you join us?"

Kamanie's heart raced. This time it wasn't out of fear, it was with excitement. She looked at her friends, who nodded and smiled. Their encouragement was like a warm embrace and a gentle nudge forward.

Later that day, Kamanie's time came to address the audience. She took a deep breath and stepped onto the stage. The spotlight shined on her, and for a moment, she felt like a star in the sky, sparkling with endless possibilities. With her heart full of confidence, she performed the song she had written from her favorite words of affirmation. When she sang, her voice was strong and clear.

Yesterday,
Questions used to
Follow my way
Questions like,
What's wrong with me?
Am I enough?
And, is it really okay to be different?

Tomorrow,
I've decided
The time has come
To be myself
And step out
into the world
Just as I am

On this day,
They all can say
whatever they want to say
Cause this is the day
I'm gonna be brave
Going my way
Starting a whole new wave

Being me
It opens up a secret treasure
It sets me free
Free to go and free to see
Everything
That life has given me

God made us
Different and unique
A million pieces
A world full of colors
And we can make
The most beautiful puzzle
Together

The future
Is a wide night sky
Wide enough
For us all to shine in
So the time is now
To be the star
I know you are

Remember,
You're brave
Strong
Awesome
It's true
Be yourself:
There's no one like you.

The audience clapped and cheered, their smiles reflecting the love and admiration they felt for Kamanie. As she walked off the stage, she knew that her journey to embracing her uniqueness had not only transformed her life but had also inspired others to do the same.

Years later, Kamanie went to college. She had grown into a young woman who believed in herself and her dreams. She had become a source of light for those who needed a reminder that being different was a beautiful thing.

And so, with a heart full of gratitude and a spirit that soared, Kamanie looked ahead to the future, ready to face whatever challenges and joys that lay ahead. For she knew that as long as she stayed true to herself and embraced her uniqueness, there was a world of endless possibilities waiting to be discovered.

And they all lived happily ever after, in a world where being different was celebrated, and each person's uniqueness was like a brilliant star in the vast sky of life.

THE END